Armenia

 **Australia**

 Austria

 **Azerbaijan**

 Bahamas

 **Bahrain**

 Bangladesh

 **Bosnia-Herzegovina**

 Botswana

 Brazil

 Brunei

 Bulgaria

 Burkina Faso

 Burma (Myanmar)

 Chile

 China

 **Colombia**

 Comoros

 Congo

 Congo (Democratic Republic)

 Costa Rica

 Dominican Republic

 East Timor

 Ecuador

 Egypt

 El Salvador

 Equatorial Guinea

 Eritrea

 Georgia

 Germany

 Ghana

 Greece

 **Greenland**

 Grenada

 Guatemala

 India

 Indonesia

 Iran

 **Iraq**

 Ireland

 **Israel**

 **Italy**

 Korea, North

 Korea, South

Kosovo

Kuwait

Kyrgyzstan

 **Laos**

Latvia

PHILIP'S

Infant School Atlas

DAVID WRIGHT AND RACHEL NOONAN

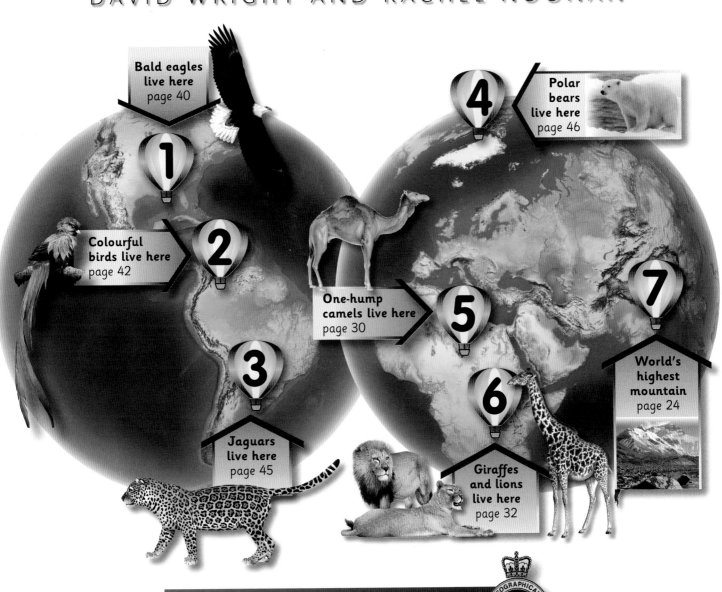

Bald eagles live here page 40

Polar bears live here page 46

Colourful birds live here page 42

One-hump camels live here page 30

World's highest mountain page 24

Jaguars live here page 45

Giraffes and lions live here page 32

IN ASSOCIATION WITH
THE ROYAL GEOGRAPHICAL SOCIETY
WITH THE INSTITUTE OF BRITISH GEOGRAPHERS

About this Atlas

Message to Adults

Children love discovering new things . . . this atlas has hundreds of new things to discover! Some will even be a surprise for adults!

This is an atlas for young children to enjoy. We can't tell children everything about everywhere, but we *can* take them to some amazing places.

They will find out a lot about the geography, people, climate, plants and animals – as well as some of the problems – of our amazing world!

Don't worry about detailed understanding just yet. The numbered balloons on the maps allow the children to find the places on each map. Every numbered balloon has a corresponding picture and text about that particular *real* place.

As well as beautiful photographs and illustrations, we have included lots of wonderful postage stamps: real messages from real places! There are messages on the flags we have chosen too.

Message to Children

Welcome to this world atlas – let's explore the world together!

Our **balloon** takes you to **real places**. You can find where these places are on the **maps**. The **pictures** and **words** tell you more about each place.

You will soon discover things that most grown-ups don't know!

Meet the Authors

Both the authors are graduates who have travelled round the world. David has been to 106 countries! He was a university lecturer, and now he is an author: he has written 20 books.

His daughter Rachel works with children at her local school in Norwich, UK, where her 3 children go to school.

When you've visited all the places in this atlas, you can meet David again and find out more about our world in **Philip's Children's Atlas**, written for 7 to 12 year olds by David and his wife Jill.

David Wright

Rachel Noonan

First published in Great Britain in 2009 by Philip's, a division of Octopus Publishing Group Limited (www.octopusbooks.co.uk)
Carmelite House, 50 Victoria Embankment, London EC4Y 0DZ
An Hachette UK Company (www.hachette.co.uk)

To Florence, Molly and Isaac
Text © 2009 David Wright and Rachel Noonan
Maps © 2015 Philip's
First published 2009. Second edition 2015.

Cartography by Philip's

A CIP catalogue record for this book is available from the British Library.

ISBN 978-1-84907-396-7

David Wright and Rachel Noonan have asserted their moral rights under the Copyright, Designs and Patents Act, 1988, to be identified as the authors of this work.

Printed in Hong Kong

Details of other Philip's titles and services can be found on our website at: **www.philips-maps.co.uk**

Contents

Philip's and the Royal Geographical Society

This Philip's atlas displays the logo of the **Royal Geographical Society** (with the **Institute of British Geographers**). The Royal Geographical Society supports education, teaching, research and expeditions. The role of 'promoting public understanding of geography' now reaches 5 to 7 year olds through this new atlas.

Philip's has been publishing good maps for over 150 years.

Find out more about the Royal Geographical Society! Visit their website at www.rgs.org – David Wright is a Fellow and a Chartered Geographer of the RGS.

Our Planet in Space

Space is huge! This picture shows the **planets** in our **Solar System**. These planets go round our Sun. But if you look at the sky at night you can see hundreds of **stars**. The stars you see are mostly other suns far, far away.

Sun

Mercury

Venus

Earth

Mars

Jupiter

Saturn

Uranus

Neptune

How long does it take for the planets to go round the Sun? They are all different. **Earth** takes **365 days** (1 year). **Mercury** only takes **88 Earth-days**, but **Neptune** takes **165 Earth-years** to circle the Sun!

Did you know?
The planets of the Solar System are very different sizes, and the Sun is huge! If the **Sun** was the size of a basketball then **Jupiter** (the biggest planet) would be the size of a pea, and the **Earth** would be smaller than a full stop!

8 planets circle the Sun. How can you remember the planets? Here is a funny sentence to help you. Can you think of an even funnier sentence to help you remember the order of the planets, using the first letter of each planet?

Mercury	My	M..........
Venus	Very	V...........
Earth	Excellent	E...........
Mars	Mother	M..........
Jupiter	Just	J...........
Saturn	Served	S...........
Uranus	Us	U..........
Neptune	Noodles	N..........

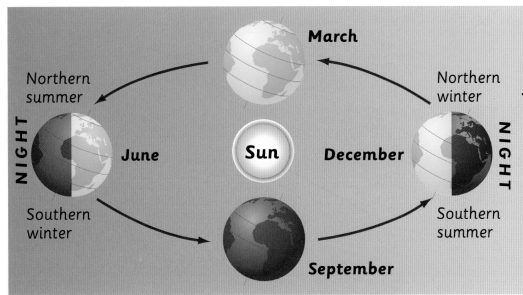

March

Northern summer

June

NIGHT

Southern winter

Sun

December

September

Northern winter

NIGHT

Southern summer

Winter is when our part of the Earth is **tilted away from the Sun**, and gets **less sunlight** and **heat**. **Summer** is when our part of the Earth is **tilted to get more sunlight** and **heat**. Tropical lands get the most heat from the Sun; Arctic lands get the least heat.

Can you be the Earth going round the Sun?
Use a ball. Spin it all the way round. This is one day. Now get a friend to stand still – they can be the Sun. Walk all the way round your friend spinning the world **365 times**!
This is one year!

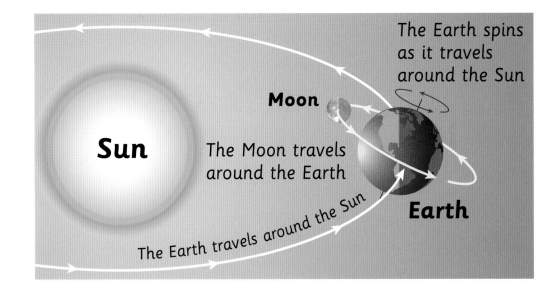

The Earth spins as it travels around the Sun

Moon

Sun

The Moon travels around the Earth

The Earth travels around the Sun

Earth

Our planet is so beautiful!
Can you find where **YOU** live? Find the names of the continents on pages 10–11.

What makes Earth such a GOOD planet to live on?
The **Sun** makes us warm. We've got **land** to live on. We've got **soil** for crops. We've got **air** to breathe. We've got **water** to drink. We've got **coal**, **oil**, **sun** and **wind** for energy. We've got **friends** too! Can you think of more good reasons to live here?

Our Planet Earth is ...

1 ... so beautiful!

Imagine you are in a spacecraft; you look out of the window and see **THIS!**

Wow! You can see blue **oceans**, white **clouds** and green **land**.

2 ... so varied

Our artist has put 4 amazing places on 1 picture!
Can you find...

... cold, icy Antarctica (find out more on page **47**),

... hot, sandy desert (see page **30**),

... tall fir forest by a lake (see page **20**),

... a city with skyscrapers (see page **29**)?

CAN YOU FIND...
North America? (Find out more on page **38**.)
South America?
(See page **44**.)
Some islands?
(See page **43**.)

3 ... a sphere

An easy shape to understand. If you've caught a ball, you know the shape of our planet! (See page **4**.)

4 ... so light – and so dark!

In one whole year every place on Earth has **equal time in light and darkness** – half and half. [**It's true!**]

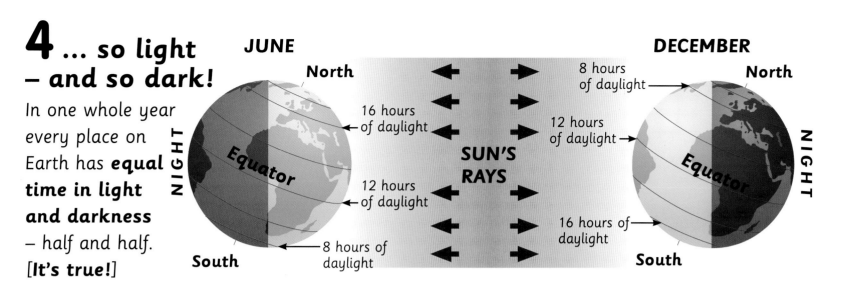

JUNE

North

16 hours of daylight

Equator

12 hours of daylight

8 hours of daylight

South

NIGHT

SUN'S RAYS

DECEMBER

8 hours of daylight

North

12 hours of daylight

Equator

16 hours of daylight

South

NIGHT

It is so easy to work out the shortest routes for aeroplanes!

To find the shortest route by air on a globe:

1 Find your start point (**A**).

2 Find your end point (**B**).

3 Put a piece of string between your start point and end point.

4 Pull the string tight – and that's the shortest route!

Surprise! From **London** (**A**) to **Los Angeles** (**B**), the shortest route goes over **Greenland**!

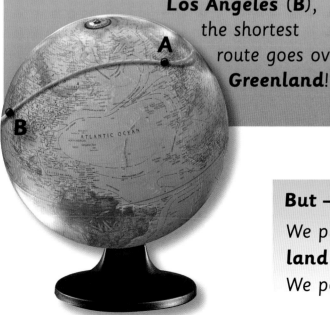

But it is so difficult to put the world on a flat map!

Find out more on page **8**. This stamp from **Canada** shows one way of keeping shapes right – do you like it?

COMMONWEALTH DAY
JOUR DU COMMONWEALTH
1983/03/14

$2 CANADA

But – we pollute our planet in lots of ways.

We put rubbish on the **land** and in the **sea**.

We pollute the **air**.

We spoil our **soils**.

We cut down **trees**.

We catch too many **fish**.

Understanding Maps

The best way to understand maps is to **USE maps!**

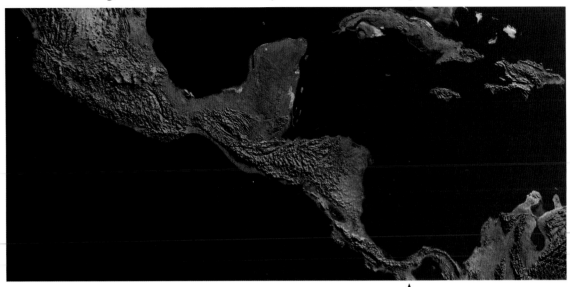

This is a **SATELLITE IMAGE** of Central America. ↑

This is a **MAP** of Central America. ↑

Here is an image taken from a satellite in space. Look at the image and the map. Can you find: the **land**, the **sea**, **islands**, a **lake**, and some **mountains**?

Here is a map of the same places. **Can you spot some differences?** A map is like a picture taken from the air. A map can tell you a lot more than a picture: the names of cities, rivers and mountains, and borders where countries begin and end.

The satellite image does not show any borders.
Can you see which **map colour** is used for the **sea** and the **rivers**?*
Can you see which **map colour** is used for **borders**?*

Maps can be of very big places, or of small places.
Can you draw a map of your bedroom? A globe is a map of the whole world. Maps are usually flat, but a **globe** is a map and it is a **sphere**!

What can maps tell us?

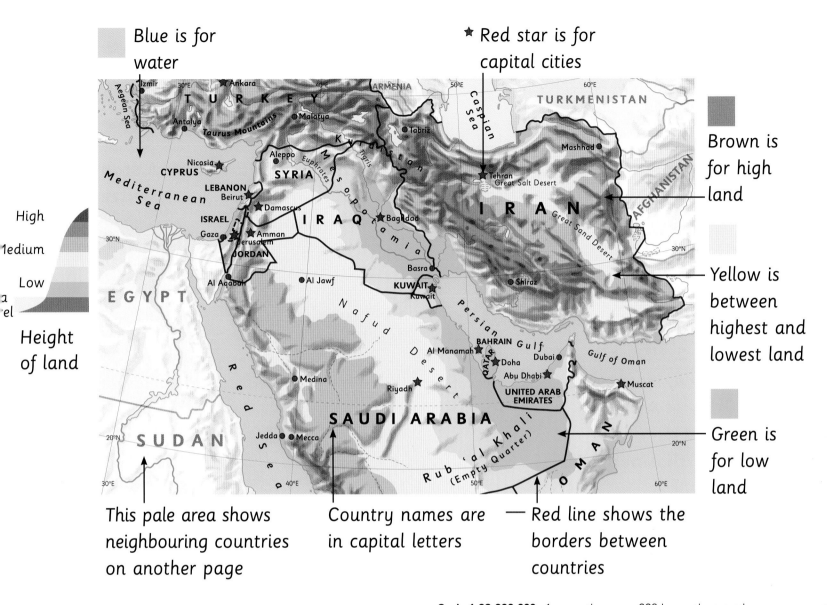

Blue is for water

★ Red star is for capital cities

Brown is for high land

Yellow is between highest and lowest land

Green is for low land

High
Medium
Low

Height of land

This pale area shows neighbouring countries on another page

Country names are in capital letters

— Red line shows the borders between countries

This is the scale bar. It tells you how far **1 centimetre** on the map is on the real world!

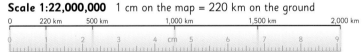

Scale 1:22,000,000   1 cm on the map = 220 km on the ground

0   220 km   500 km   1,000 km   1,500 km   2,000 km

0   1   2   3   4 cm   5   6   7   8   9

Where in the world?
This little map of the world is on every page. It shows you where in the world the big map is. It also shows you how big that bit of the world is.
Use a globe as well! Only globes always have the right size and the right shape for all parts of the world.

Map makers (cartographers) are so careful to make maps accurate that you can even use a map to find out how far it is from one place to another place.

Oceans, Continents and Countries

A stamp from Switzerland. This is the badge of the United Nations.

This map shows our whole world.

Our 7 continents are named in big, bold letters like this: **EUROPE**. Our world has **4 oceans** – can you name them? A..., A..., I..., and P....

The **'Top 10' countries** are named on this map. These countries have the most people.

Find the **blue** people with **white** numbers. China has the most people, so is number 1. India is 2, USA is 3 and so on. Most of the 'Top 10' are in Asia, but can you find ...

ONE in **North America**?* [This is easy!]

ONE in **South America**?*

ONE in **Africa**?*

'TOP 10' COUNTRIES:

1. **China** 1,356 million people
2. **India** 1,236 million people
3. **USA** 319 million people
4. **Indonesia** 254 million people
5. **Brazil** 203 million people
6. **Pakistan** 196 million people
7. **Nigeria** 177 million people
8. **Bangladesh** 166 million people
9. **Russia** 142 million people
10. **Japan** 127 million people

The **Atlantic Ocean** is **7 times bigger** than the **Arctic Ocean**.

The **Pacific Ocean** is **HUGE! GIGANTIC! ENORMOUS!** It is bigger than **ALL** the world's land!

10 *Find answers on page 48

The 'BIG 6' countries.
①②③④⑤⑥
There are 6 very big countries – our map shows them all. We can all see the biggest country: **Russia**! It is over 17 million square kilometres in area.

'BIG 6': a list of all the countries with more than 4 million square kilometres of land.
1. **Russia** Over 17 million
2. **Canada** Nearly 10 million
3. **USA** Over 9 million
4. **China** Over 9 million
5. **Brazil** Over 8 million
6. **Australia** Over 7 million

The 'snip' at the bottom of the map allows continents to be the right **SIZE** and the right **SHAPE**. Many world maps make the cold lands too **BIG** and the hot lands too **SMALL**. Our map gets it right!

A stamp from Fiji. The Pacific Ocean is in the middle!

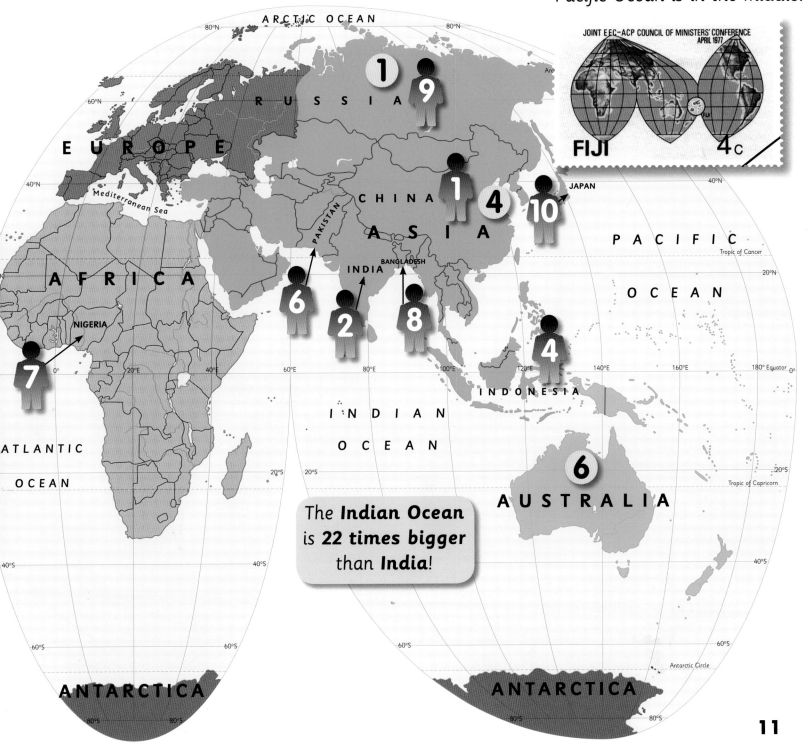

The **Indian Ocean** is **22 times bigger** than **India**!

11

Discover... the British Isles

1 Can you see the houses of Parliament and Big Ben? This is where the government of the United Kingdom meets to make new laws.

This giant wheel takes you up, so that you can see London from the air.

2 These amazing stones were put up without diggers or cranes. This is **Stonehenge**; it was built by the people who lived in Britain about 4,000 years ago!

3 This is a little train for big people! Now it carries tourists, but it used to carry slate. **100 years ago** there was a lot of mining in **Wales**. Welsh slate makes really good roofs.

4 This bridge is so amazing! This picture is on a £1 coin! It was built for trains by the Victorians over 100 years ago. The **Forth Bridge** was the first big bridge made of steel.

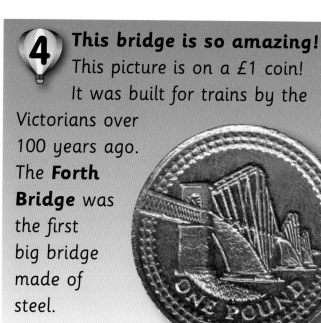

6 This cross is special. It is an old Celtic cross in **Ireland**. Can you draw the pattern carved on it?

5 **Scotland** has big mountains and great wildlife. This is **Ben Nevis**, the highest mountain in the British Isles. **Can you** see what the osprey will have for dinner?

To the North Pole page 46

Did you know? The Shetland Islands are much nearer to **NORWAY** than to London! (See map on page 15.)

The Union Jack...

England + Scotland + St Patrick

...is made from **THREE FLAGS**!

This way to Canada page 39

7 **The flag of Ireland:** Green for Catholics; Orange for Protestants; and White in the middle for peace in Ireland.

This way to Western Europe page 15

This way to the Mediterranean page 17

Scale 1:5,500,000   1 cm on the map = 55 km on the ground

0   55 km 100 km   200 km   300 km   400 km   500 km

0   1   2   3   4   cm 5   6   7   8   9

Map labels:

ATLANTIC OCEAN

North Sea

Shetland Islands

Lerwick

Orkney Islands

Kirkwall

Cape Wrath

Thurso

Lewis

Stornoway

St Kilda

Outer Hebrides

Portree
Skye

Inner Hebrides

North West Highlands

Inverness

Aviemore

Aberdeen

5 Fort William Ben Nevis

SCOTLAND

Mull

Oban

Stirling

Dundee

4 Edinburgh Firth of Forth

Glasgow

Clyde

Arran

Southern Uplands

Berwick-upon-Tweed

Dumfries

Carlisle

Tyne

Newcastle-upon-Tyne

UNITED KINGDOM

North Channel

Londonderry
NORTHERN IRELAND

Donegal

Sligo

6 Belfast

Isle of Man

Douglas

Scarborough

York

Leeds

Pennines

Blackpool

IRELAND

Galway

7

Dublin

Irish Sea

Anglesey

Liverpool

Manchester

Sheffield

Lincoln

ENGLAND

Nottingham

3 Wrexham

Leicester

Norwich

Limerick

Shannon

Shrewsbury

Birmingham

Cambridge

Ipswich

Wexford

Aberystwyth WALES

Brecon

Gloucester

Oxford

1 London

Killarney

Carmarthen

Swansea

Cardiff

Severn

Bristol

Thames

2 Salisbury

Hastings

Cork

Exeter

Portsmouth
Isle of Wight

FRANCE

Plymouth

Penzance Truro

Isles of Scilly

English Channel

Discover...
Western Europe

1 **Over 1,000 years ago the Vikings sailed from Norway.** Viking boats were amazing. People could sail them, row them and even carry them! Vikings sailed to many lands

2 **Reindeer live in the far north.** The far north of Europe is inside the **Arctic Circle**. Find out more on page 46.

3 **Why do people decorate trees at Christmas?** The tradition of Christmas trees came from **Germany**. Now Christians all over the world decorate trees in their homes at Christmas time – the 'birthday' of Jesus.

4 **The European Union has its head office in Belgium. SURPRISE!** The walls are made of ... **GLASS!**

What is this flag? This is the flag of the **EU** – the **European Union**. Find more EU countries on pages 17 and 19. People travel from all over Europe to **Belgium** to discuss new ideas and laws.

5 **The Arc de Triomphe is in Paris, the capital of France.** The words mean 'triumphal arch'. It lists the victories of Emperor Napoleon.

6 **Skiing is fun in the Alps in winter.** The high snowy mountains of **Switzerland** make good ski slopes in winter.

Scale 1:17,500,000   1 cm on the map = 175 km on the ground

0   175 km   500 km   1,000 km   1,500 km

To the North Pole page 46

This way to Russia page 21

This way to USA page 41

To Africa page 31

Barents Sea

Tromso
Lapland
RUSSIA
Kokkola
FINLAND
Helsinki
ESTONIA
RUSSIA
LATVIA
LITHUANIA
RUSSIA
BELARUS

ICELAND
Reykjavik

Arctic Circle

Norwegian Sea

Trondheim
Bergen
Oslo
Stockholm

ATLANTIC

Faroe Islands

Shetland Islands

OCEAN

Orkney Islands

Inverness
Aberdeen

Hebrides

Glasgow   Edinburgh

North Sea
DENMARK   Copenhagen
Baltic Sea

Belfast
IRELAND
Dublin
Limerick
Cork

UNITED KINGDOM

Manchester

Birmingham

Cardiff
London
Plymouth

NETHERLANDS
Amsterdam
Hamburg
Berlin
POLAND
UKRAINE

Brussels   Bonn
BELGIUM
GERMANY
Frankfurt
CZECH REPUBLIC
SLOVAK REPUBLIC

English Channel
Channel Islands

Luxembourg
LUXEMBOURG
Seine
Strasbourg
Rhine
Munich
Salzburg
Danube   Vienna
AUSTRIA
HUNGARY

Paris

FRANCE

Berne
SWITZERLAND
LIECHTENSTEIN
Geneva
SLOVENIA
CROATIA
ROMANIA

Bay of Biscay

Bordeaux

Rhône

ITALY
BOSNIA-HERZEGOVINA
SERBIA

Adriatic Sea

KOSOVO

Toulouse
Avignon
Nice
Marseilles
MONTENEGRO
MACEDONIA
ALBANIA

Pyrenees

Corsica

SPAIN
PORTUGAL

Mediterranean
Tyrrhenian Sea
Ionian Sea
GREECE

To Africa page 31

MOROCCO
ALGERIA
TUNISIA
MALTA
Sea

15

Discover... Mediterranean Europe

1 **A procession to remember Jesus in Burgos.**
The days before Easter in **Spain** are called **Semana Santa** (Holy Week). There are processions every day. People feel sad but on Easter Day everyone feels happy again.

2 **This is the flag of Slovenia:** the shield shows the three peaks of Mount Triglav.

3 **The Colosseum in Rome.** Lots of buildings in **Rome** were built by the Romans over **2,000 years ago**. Now millions of people live here, so there are lots of new buildings and cars too.

4 **This is a new bridge that looks old.** The old bridge was blown up in the war in **Bosnia** in 1993. Now there is peace – and the bridge has been built again, just like the old bridge.

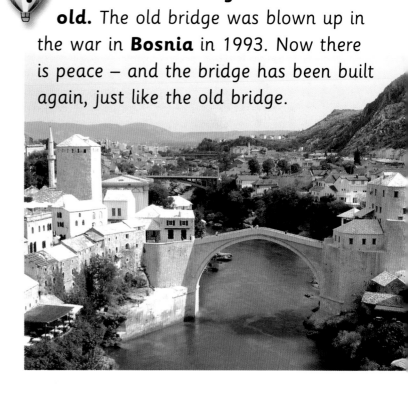

5 This temple is over **2,000 years old.** It is called the **Parthenon.** It is in **Athens**, the capital city of Greece. How many columns can you count? Do you know any words that come from Greek words? Clue: find words with 'ph': they come from Greece!

6 **What is growing here?** These are **olive trees** in Crete. Olives and grapes grow well in Mediterranean lands. Why? Remember the 5 Ws: '**Warm Wet Westerly Winds** in **Winter**'.

7 There are lots of fish in the **Mediterranean Sea.** Fish is good food and tourists like to eat fish. But there are two problems: over-fishing and pollution. This photo shows a fish shop in **Naples**, **Italy**.

Scale 1:15,000,000   1 cm on the map = 150 km on the ground

This way to the USA page 41

This way to Russia page 21

Discover...
Eastern Europe

1 This looks like hard work! This horse is pulling a plough in **Poland**; the farmer is keeping it straight. Soon there will be good cabbages to eat. Try looking for Polish food in shops – can you find **pierogi** or **golagki**?

2 Which ALPHABET or АЛФАВИТ?
Belarus and Ukraine use the Russian Cyrillic alphabet. Try writing your name using the key below!

3 Children in Ukraine are folk-dancing. It's fun – and a good way to find out about history.
Did you know? Ukraine is bigger than France!

4 Skiers catch this train. They travel through snowy forests to the Carpathian Mountains in the **Slovak Republic**.

А	Б	В	Г	Д	Е	Ё	Ж	З	И	Й	К	Л	М	Н	О	П	Р	С	Т	У	Ф	Х	Ц	Ч	Ш	Щ	Ю	Я
A	B	V	G	D	E	YO	ZH	Z	I	Y	K	L	M	N	O	P	R	S	T	U	F	KH	TS	CH	SH	SHCH	YU	YA

1987

Today

Spot the differences!

Lots of the countries of Eastern Europe were not on the map in 1987. Can you find some?

Spot **6** new countries* – **well done!**

Spot **8** – **excellent!**

Spot **10** – **FANTASTIC!**

5 The River Danube passes through **8 countries**.

It flows from Germany to the Black Sea. This boat **pushes** big barges.

Scale 1:16,000,000 1 cm on the map = 160 km on the ground

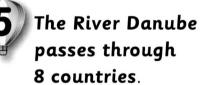

0   160 km   500 km   1,000 km   1,500 km   2,000 km

This way to the Arctic page 46

Can you find 2 big seas beginning with B?*

This way to Russia page 21

To Africa page 31

Discover...
Russia and its Neighbours

1 Kamchatka has lots of volcanoes!
They are part of the Pacific Ring of Fire — the volcanoes all round the Pacific Ocean. We are still in **Russia**, but we're nearer to North America than to Moscow!

3 Lake Baikal is the deepest lake in the world. Winters are so cold here that they laid the Trans-Siberian railway across the frozen lake! Now the railway goes round the edge.

Russian dolls are made of wood — they are **NOT** cuddly!

2 Trams are good for travel in cities. Many Russian cities have trams, with rails and electric wires.

4 The world's biggest forest!
The forest of Siberian Russia is far bigger than any other forest. This is a **coniferous forest**: the trees have cones. The lake is frozen in winter.

5 The tundra of Northern Russia is very cold in winter – but reindeer like it! In summer it is marshy because the ground underneath is still frozen. But in some places, there is deep melting in summer.

6 A beautiful mosque in Samarkand, Uzbekistan. Most people in Uzbekistan are Muslims.

7 The Caspian Sea is shared by 5 countries. Can you name some of them?* In wet years the sea grows bigger; in dry years it is smaller. Seals live here. This seal is on the ice.

15 TÜRKMENISTAN
Phoca caspica • Düwleň
WWF
1993

Scale 1:40 000 000 1 cm on the map = 400 km on the ground

| 0 | 410 km | 1,000 km | 2,000 km | 3,000 km | 4,000 km | 5,000 km |

This way to the Arctic page 46

To the USA page 41

To Eastern Europe page 19

To India and Southern Asia page 25

To Middle East page 23

GREENLAND

Norwegian Sea
Arctic Circle
NORWAY
SWEDEN
FINLAND
Barents Sea
Murmansk
White Sea
Archangel
ESTONIA
LATVIA
St Petersburg
LITHUANIA
BELARUS
Smolensk
Moscow
Nizhniy Novgorod
Saratov
Ufa
Yekaterinburg
Orenburg
Volgograd
Rostov
Astrakhan
Elbrus
GEORGIA Tbilisi
ARMENIA AZER-BAIJAN
Yerevan Baku
TURKEY
IRAQ
IRAN
Caspian Sea
KAZAKHSTAN
Aral Sea
Syrdarya
UZBEKISTAN
Urgench
TURKMENISTAN
Ashkhabad
Samarkand
Dushanbe TAJIKISTAN
Bishkek KYRGYZSTAN
Tashkent
Alma Ata
Lake Balkhash
Astana
Omsk
Novosibirsk
Tomsk
Krasnoyarsk
Irkutsk
Lake Baikal
MONGOLIA
Tian Shan
Altai
CHINA
ARCTIC OCEAN
Laptev Sea
Taimyr Peninsula
Yenisei
Norilsk
Siberia
Verkhoyansk Range
Lena
Yakutsk
Kolyma Range
Kolyma
East Siberian Sea
Bering Strait
Arctic Circle
Bering Sea
Kamchatka
Okhotsk
Sea of Okhotsk
Sakhalin
Stanovoy Range
Amur
Khabarovsk
Vladivostok
Sea of Japan
NORTH KOREA
SOUTH KOREA
JAPAN
PACIFIC OCEAN
Yablonovyy Range
Chita
RUSSIA
Ural Mountains
Ob
Irtysh
Nizhnevartovsk
Don
Volga

Discover...
the Middle East

The Dome of the Rock is an Islamic monument. Before that there was probably a Christian church and before that a Roman temple and a Jewish temple.

1 **Jerusalem means 'Place of Peace'.** It is a holy city for 3 big religions: Islam, Judaism and Christianity.

Religion	Symbol	Holy day
Islam	☪	Friday
Judaism	✡	Saturday
Christianity	✝	Sunday

2 **Petra in Jordan was once a 'lost city'.** Now the ruins are visited by thousands of people! **Amazing!** This temple was carved out of solid rock!

Did you know?
The Middle East is the only place where **3 continents** meet. Can you name them?* The map on page 23 will help you.

3 **Iraq has old and new ruins.** The old ruins are from some of the oldest cities on Earth! The new ruins are from wars.

4 **Muslims all over the world pray facing Mecca.** One of the 5 pillars of Islam is to pray 5 times a day; another is to visit Mecca at least once.

5 **Much of the Middle East is very dry,** so irrigating (watering) the land is very important. This stamp from **Oman** shows an irrigation channel. What else can you see in the picture?*

SULTANATE OF OMAN
130 BAISA
INTERNATIONAL ENVIRONMENT DAY

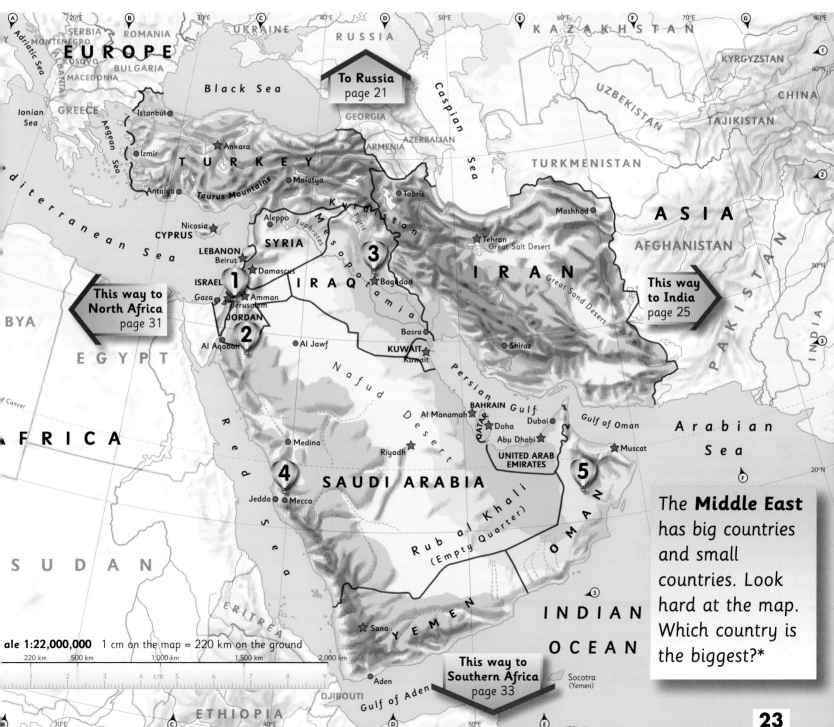

To Russia
page 21

This way to North Africa
page 31

This way to India
page 25

This way to Southern Africa
page 33

The **Middle East** has big countries and small countries. Look hard at the map. Which country is the biggest?*

ale 1:22,000,000   1 cm on the map = 220 km on the ground
220 km   500 km   1,000 km   1,500 km   2,000 km

23

Discover...
India and Southern Asia

1 **Afghanistan has high mountains, dry deserts and lonely ruins.** But wars have made it a very hard place to live in.

Did you know?
3 religions started in India – **Hinduism**, **Sikhism** and **Buddhism**. Lots of different languages are spoken in India – and many of them have their own alphabet. **Islam** is the main religion in Afghanistan, Pakistan and Bangladesh.

2 **Pakistan is mostly desert**, yet it has more people than any country in Europe or Africa. How can so many people live here? The **River Indus** brings water all year from the high mountains.

POSTAGE · PAISA 10
RICE
WE EXPORT
THE BEST
PAKISTAN
পাকিস্তান · پاکستان

4 **Yaks are amazing animals!** People come to the Himalayas to climb the highest moutains in the world. Yaks help to carry all the things the people need. All yaks need is water, grass and their thick fur!

3 **This is the Taj Mahal.** Over 1,000 elephants were used to bring stone to build this beautiful building.

6 In Sri Lanka, tea grows in high mountains – where the days are hot and the nights are cold. Tea-pickers take 2 leaves from each stalk and put them in the baskets on their backs.

5 Mumbai (Bombay) is a big city. Some people here are rich, but many are very poor.

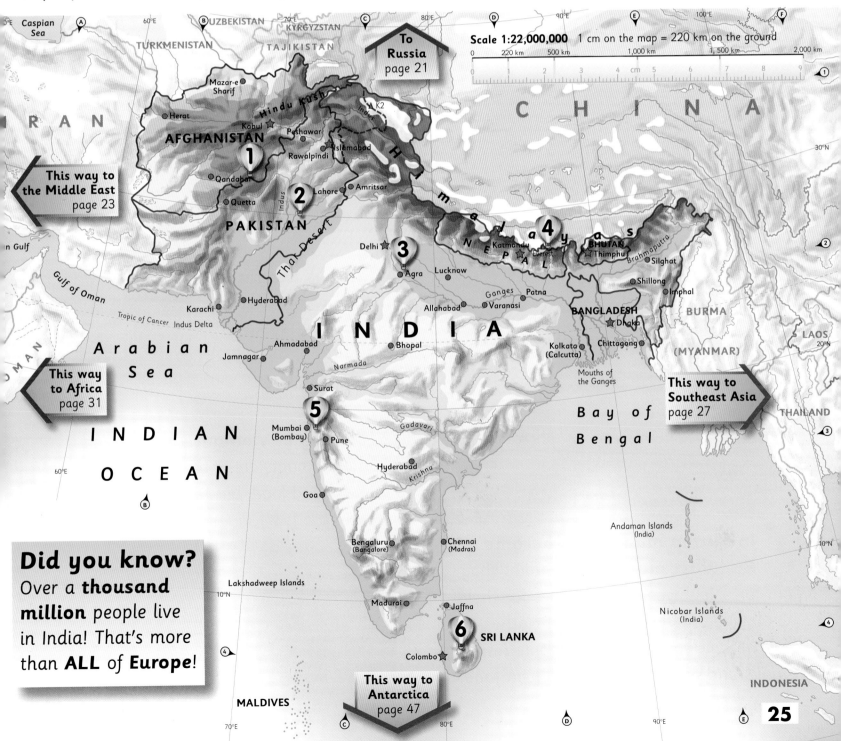

To Russia page 21

Scale 1:22,000,000   1 cm on the map = 220 km on the ground

0   220 km   500 km   1,000 km   1,500 km   2,000 km

Caspian Sea

TURKMENISTAN

UZBEKISTAN

KYRGYZSTAN

TAJIKISTAN

Mazar-e Sharif

I R A N

Herat

Hindu Kush

K2

AFGHANISTAN

Kabul

Peshawar

Islamabad

Rawalpindi

1

This way to the Middle East page 23

Qandahar

2 Lahore   Amritsar

Quetta

PAKISTAN

Indus

Thar Desert

C H I N A

H i m a l a y a s

Delhi   **3**

NEPAL   **4**   Katmandu   BHUTAN   Brahmaputra

Everest   Thimphu

Agra   Lucknow

Silghat

Shillong

Ganges   Patna

Imphal

n Gulf

Gulf of Oman

Karachi   Hyderabad

Allahabad   Varanasi

BANGLADESH

Tropic of Cancer   Indus Delta

Dhaka

BURMA

I N D I A

Ahmadabad   Bhopal

Kolkata (Calcutta)   Chittagong

(MYANMAR)

A r a b i a n

Jamnagar

Narmada

Mouths of the Ganges

LAOS

This way to Africa page 31

S e a

Surat   **5**

Godavari

Bay of

This way to Southeast Asia page 27

OMAN

I N D I A N

Mumbai (Bombay)   Pune

Bengal

THAILAND

O C E A N

Hyderabad

Krishna

60°E

Goa

Andaman Islands (India)

Did you know? Over a **thousand million** people live in India! That's more than **ALL** of Europe!

Bengaluru (Bangalore)   Chennai (Madras)

Lakshadweep Islands

10°N

Madurai   Jaffna

Nicobar Islands (India)

6   SRI LANKA

Colombo

This way to Antarctica page 47

MALDIVES

INDONESIA

Discover...
Southeast Asia

Rice is planted in flooded fields. But water runs down hills! So – how do you grow rice on a slope? Look at Balloon 6 for a clue.

2 **A beautiful palace in Bangkok**, the capital city of Thailand. How many spires can you count?

3 **This is the flag of Cambodia.** In the centre is a drawing of the temple of Angkor Wat.

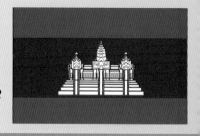

4 **Fishing in Vietnam** – these round fishing boats are in the South China Sea. Fish is good food, but too much fishing causes too few fish.

1 **In Burma many boys become Buddhist monks.** Sometimes they join for a few weeks, sometimes for their whole lives. They wear special clothes, like the boy in this picture. People respect monks and are happy to give them food.

5 Where does rubber come from?

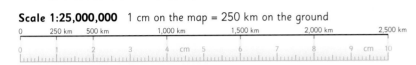

This is a rubber tree in a plantation in **Malaysia**. The rubber is the sap of the tree. Some can be 'tapped' and collected.

GETAH
Hevea brasiliensis

WILAYAH PERSEKUTUAN
Malaysia 15¢

6 Can you see where people have cut steps into the hill?
These are flat places (called terraces) to plant rice and hold the water. This means that lots of rice can be grown even on steep slopes.

Scale 1:25,000,000   1 cm on the map = 250 km on the ground

0	250 km	500 km	1,000 km	1,500 km	2,000 km	2,500 km

| 0 | 1 | 2 | 3 | 4 | cm | 5 | 6 | 7 | 8 | 9 | cm | 10 |

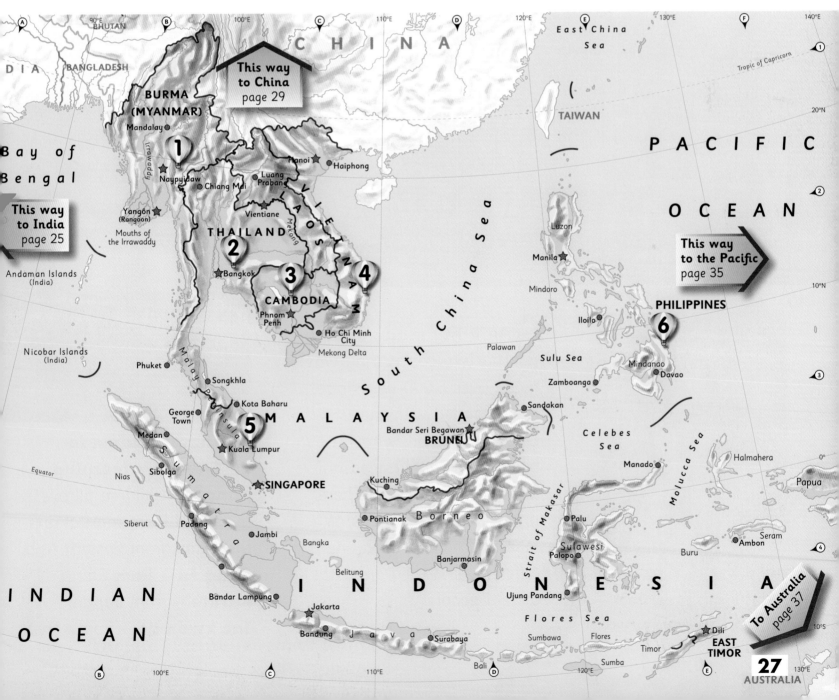

CHINA

BHUTAN

BANGLADESH

This way to China page 29

BURMA (MYANMAR)

Mandalay

Irrawaddy

1

Naypyidaw

Chiang Mai

Luang Prabang

Hanoi · Haiphong

LAOS

VIETNAM

East China Sea

TAIWAN

Tropic of Capricorn

20°E

90°E   100°E   110°E   120°E   130°E   140°E

A   B   C   D   E   F

PACIFIC

OCEAN

Bay of Bengal

This way to India page 25

Yangon (Rangoon)

Vientiane

Mouths of the Irrawaddy

THAILAND

Mekong

2

Bangkok

3

CAMBODIA

Phnom Penh

4

Andaman Islands (India)

Nicobar Islands (India)

Phuket

Songkhla

Mekong Delta

Ho Chi Minh City

South China Sea

Palawan

Luzon

Manila

Mindoro

This way to the Pacific page 35

PHILIPPINES

Iloilo

6

Sulu Sea

Mindanao

Davao

Zamboanga

Kota Baharu

George Town

5

MALAYSIA

Bandar Seri Begawan

BRUNEI

Sandakan

Celebes Sea

Manado

Halmahera

Medan

Kuala Lumpur

Kuching

Molucca Sea

Papua

Equator

Nias

Sibolga

Sumatra

SINGAPORE

Borneo

Pontianak

Strait of Makasar

Palu

Sulawesi

Palopo

Seram

Ambon

Buru

Siberut

Padang

Jambi

Bangka

Banjarmasin

Ujung Pandang

INDONESIA

To Australia page 37

INDIAN

OCEAN

Bandar Lampung

Belitung

Jakarta

Bandung

Java

Surabaya

Bali

Flores Sea

Sumbawa

Flores

Timor

Sumba

EAST TIMOR

Dili

10°S

100°E   110°E   120°E   130°E

B   C   D   E

10°N

0°

Discover...
China and its Neighbours

1 The Bactrian camel (Asian camel) has **two humps** and can live in dry places that are hot or cold. A few wild camels still live in **Mongolia**.

2 **An army made of clay!** The Terracotta Army was made over 2,000 years ago. It was buried with the Emperor of Quin, who believed he would need an army in the after-life. There are over **8,000 figures** of men and horses! Each one is different, and they are as big as real people!

3 These children in China are learning **Kung Fu.** Children all over the world learn martial arts that came from Eastern Asia. **Kung Fu** – from China; **Karate** – from Japan; **Tae kwon do** – from Korea.

4 **China has many big cities** with big buildings and factories where lots of people live and work. Lots of things are made in China and sold all over the world.

6 **Japan has beautiful old palaces**, and flowering cherry trees in spring.

5

North Korea flag

Korea is split into 2 countries: North Korea and South Korea.

South Korea flag

Scale 1:25,000,000 1 cm on the map = 250 km on the ground

| 0 | 250 km | 500 km | 1,000 km | 1,500 km | 2,000 km | 2,500 km | 3,000 km |

| 0 | 1 | 2 | 3 | 4 cm | 5 | 6 | 7 | 8 | 9 cm | 10 | 11 | 12 |

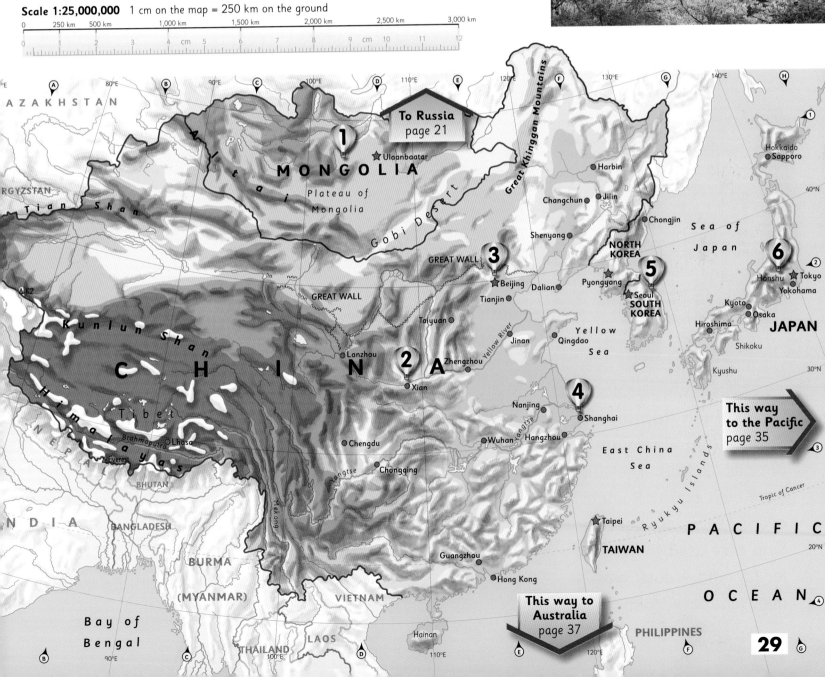

To Russia
page 21

A 80°E   B 90°E   C 100°E   D 110°E   E   120°E   F 130°E   G   140°E   H

AZAKHSTAR

1

MONGOLIA
☆ Ulaanbaatar

Plateau of
Mongolia

Gobi Desert

Great Khinggan Mountains

Hokkaido
● Sapporo

● Harbin

Changchun ● Jilin

Shenyang ●   ● Chongjin

Sea of
Japan

40°N

GRGYZSTAN

Tian Shan

Altai

GREAT WALL   **3**

GREAT WALL

☆ Beijing   Dalian

Tianjin

Taiyuan

NORTH
KOREA

Pyongyang ☆

5

Seoul ☆
SOUTH
KOREA

6

Honshu ● Tokyo
Yokohama

Kyoto
● Osaka

Hiroshima

JAPAN

Shikoku

Kunlun Shan

C   H   I   N   A

Lanzhou ●

2

Zhengzhou ●

Yellow River

Jinan ●

Qingdao ●

Yellow
Sea

Kyushu

30°N

Xian ●

Himalayas

Tibet

Brahmaputra ○ Lhasa

○ Everest

NEPAL

Chengdu ●

Chongqing ●

Yangtse

Nanjing ●

4

● Shanghai

Wuhan ●   Hangzhou ●

East China
Sea

Ryukyu Islands

**This way
to the Pacific**
page 35

BHUTAN

Mekong

Yangtse

NDIA

BANGLADESH

BURMA

(MYANMAR)

VIETNAM

Bay of
Bengal

LAOS

THAILAND

Hainan

Guangzhou ●

● Hong Kong

☆ Taipei

TAIWAN

Tropic of Cancer

PACIFIC

20°N

OCEAN

**This way to
Australia**
page 37

PHILIPPINES

B 90°E   C 100°E   D 110°E   E 120°E   F   G

Discover...
North and West Africa

1 **Egypt is an incredible country.** The pyramids are here, and there are lots of big temples too.
Can you ... find the **River Nile** on the map?

An oasis in the desert. Deserts are so dry that hardly any people, animals or plants can live there. But where there is **water** there is life.

What makes a camel so good at living in deserts?
Their **thick fur** keeps camels cool in the day and warm at night. Their **wide feet** stop them sinking into loose sand and stones. Their **nostrils** shut so sand cannot blow in. And they can last a long time with **no water**!

2 **A ruined Roman city in Libya.** There are lots of ruins like this. The cities were built by the Romans over 2,000 years ago. The land here used to be good for farming. Wheat was then sent back to Rome.

3

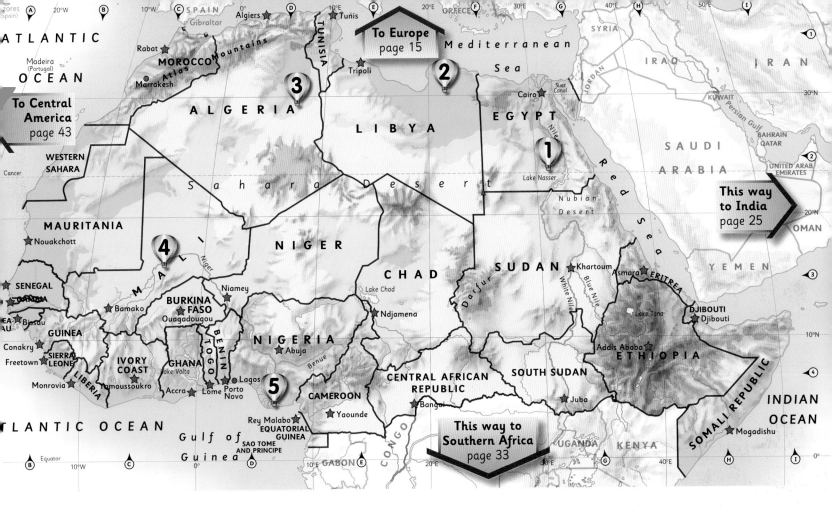

To Europe
page 15

To Central America
page 43

This way to India
page 25

This way to Southern Africa
page 33

Scale 1:34,500,000   1 cm on the map = 345 km on the ground

0   345 km   1,000 km   2,000 km   3,000 km

5 **Oil and gas in Nigeria.** Oil and gas have made a few Nigerians rich. But many people are still very poor and **pollution** is a big problem. Nigeria has more people than any country in Europe.

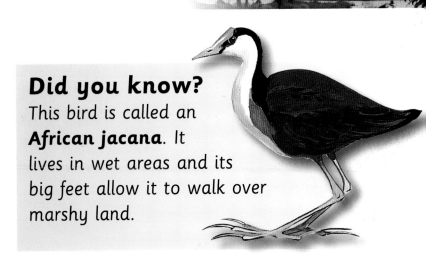

4 **A village in Mali.** These women are preparing a meal. Here there is a rainy season and a dry season. In June it rains and crops grow, but December is very hot and dry.

Did you know?
This bird is called an **African jacana**. It lives in wet areas and its big feet allow it to walk over marshy land.

Discover...
Central and Southern Africa

1 A baobab tree has such a fat trunk! The long hot dry season is no problem for a baobab as it stores water in its amazing trunk! It is sometimes called an 'upside-down' tree because the fat stumpy branches look more like roots!

2 Coffee grows best where daytime is very hot and the nights are cold. High land in Uganda is just right for growing good coffee beans!

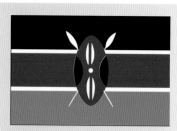

The flag of Kenya shows an African shield and 2 spears.
Black is for the African people.
Red is for the red blood of all people.
Green is for Kenya's rich agriculture.

3 These stamps from Burundi show a lion, a water buffalo, 2 hippos and a giraffe. Can you think of any other amazing animals in Africa?

REPUBLIQUE DU BURUNDI · SYNCERUS CAFFER · 1F · REPUBLIQUE DU BURUNDI · GIRAFFA CAMELOPARDALIS · REPUBLIQUE DU BURUNDI · PANTHERA LEO · 1F · REPUBLIQUE DU BURUNDI

Did you know?

There are 2 big long lakes in Africa – can you find them on the map?* Long ago the land split apart, and this '**rift valley**' became deeper and wider.

4 Elephants in the Namib Desert.

Elephants are usually found on the grasslands but these live in the desert. Lions live here too!

5 Johannesburg is a big city in South Africa.

Some hills are man-made: they are the waste rock from gold mines! The gold makes some people rich, but many people in Africa have very little money.

6 SURPRISE!

There are penguins on the south coast of South Africa – even though they are thousands of miles from Antarctica!

90c

Suid-Afrika
South Africa
DENIS MURPHY   SPHENISCUS DEMERSUS

To the rest of Africa page 31

To South America page 45

This way to Australia page 37

This way to Antarctica page 47

Scale 1:34,500,000   1 cm on the map = 345 km on the ground

345 km   1,000 km   2,000 km   3,000 km

Discover...
The Pacific

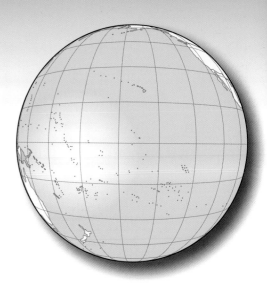

1 The Mariana Trench is the deepest part of the ocean anywhere in the world. Strange-looking creatures live in the deep ocean where daylight can never reach – like this one!

The Pacific is the biggest ocean in the world by far. It covers a third of the globe!

3 A Southern Cassowary – this large bird lives in the forests of New Guinea. But it cannot fly!

2 High islands are volcanoes. Volcanic soil is good for growing crops. But farmers must beware when a volcano is active, as it may erupt and send out lava.

Can you find these names on the maps? **Micronesia** means 'little islands'.
Melanesia means 'black islands' – the sand is black from the volcanic rock.
Polynesia means 'lots of islands'.

4 Low islands are coral islands. The sand is white! People can live on these islands but flooding from the sea is a big worry. A **coral atoll** has calm sea in the centre, but round the edges of the atoll the sea is sometimes rough.

5 Hawaii is the 50th state of the USA.

Here in the Pacific Ocean the sea is deep and warm. Many visitors come to Hawaii to enjoy the surfing.

6 Pacific islanders at work.

This canoe has been **dug out** from **ONE** forest tree by these Pacific islanders. Thousands of years ago people sailed in search of land in boats like these, using the stars to find their way.

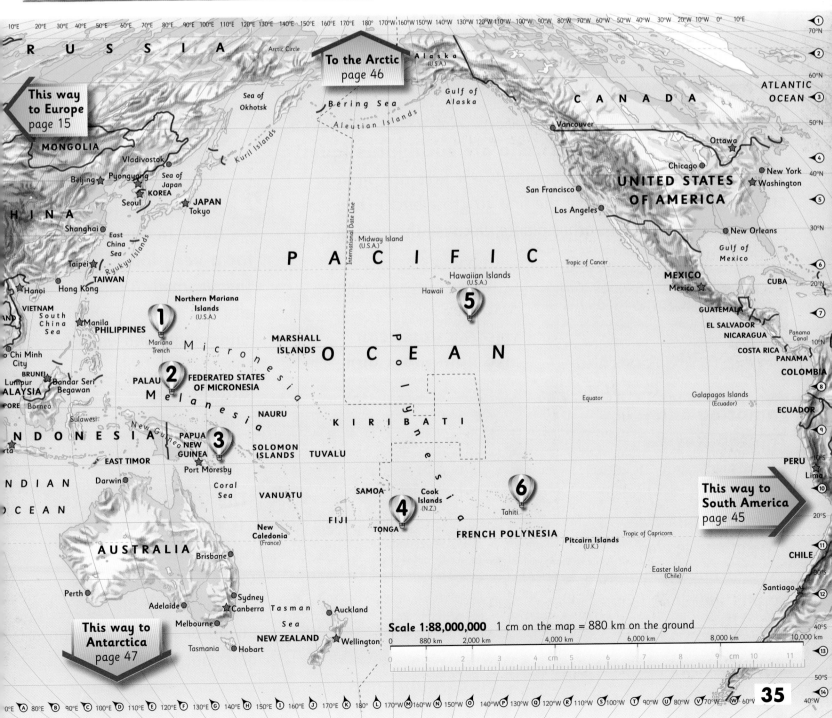

To the Arctic page 46

This way to Europe page 15

This way to South America page 45

This way to Antarctica page 47

RUSSIA

Arctic Circle

Alaska (U.S.A.)

ATLANTIC OCEAN

CANADA

Sea of Okhotsk

Bering Sea

Gulf of Alaska

Aleutian Islands

Vancouver

MONGOLIA

Vladivostok

Kuril Islands

Ottawa

Chicago

New York

Beijing Pyongyang

Sea of Japan

UNITED STATES OF AMERICA

Washington

KOREA

Seoul

JAPAN

Tokyo

San Francisco

CHINA

Shanghai

East China Sea

Los Angeles

New Orleans

Gulf of Mexico

Taipei

Ryukyu Islands

Midway Island (U.S.A.)

Tropic of Cancer

PACIFIC

Hawaiian Islands (U.S.A.)

MEXICO

Mexico

CUBA

Hanoi

Hong Kong

TAIWAN

Hawaii

Northern Mariana Islands (U.S.A.)

5

GUATEMALA

EL SALVADOR

VIETNAM

South China Sea

Manila

PHILIPPINES

1

Mariana Trench

Micronesia

MARSHALL ISLANDS

OCEAN

NICARAGUA

Panama Canal

COSTA RICA

PANAMA

Chi Minh City

BRUNEI

Bandar Seri Begawan

PALAU

2

FEDERATED STATES OF MICRONESIA

Polynesia

COLOMBIA

Lumpur

ALAYSIA

PORE

Borneo

Melanesia

NAURU

Equator

Galapagos Islands (Ecuador)

ECUADOR

Sulawesi

New Guinea

KIRIBATI

NDONESIA

rta

PAPUA NEW GUINEA

3

SOLOMON ISLANDS

TUVALU

PERU

EAST TIMOR

Port Moresby

Lima

Darwin

Coral Sea

VANUATU

SAMOA

Cook Islands (N.Z.)

4

Tahiti

6

This way to South America page 45

NDIAN

CEAN

FIJI

TONGA

FRENCH POLYNESIA

New Caledonia (France)

Pitcairn Islands (U.K.)

Tropic of Capricorn

AUSTRALIA

Brisbane

CHILE

Easter Island (Chile)

Perth

Sydney

Adelaide

Canberra

Tasman Sea

Auckland

Santiago

Melbourne

Scale 1:88,000,000 1 cm on the map = 880 km on the ground

NEW ZEALAND

Wellington

0   880 km   2,000 km   4,000 km   6,000 km   8,000 km   10,000 km

Tasmania

Hobart

International Date Line

Discover...
Australia and New Zealand

1 Lots of trees in Australia are eucalyptus (gum) trees. The hot dry climate means forest fires are often a problem, but gum trees are the first to grow back. They can take over the land from other plants, because they are quicker to grow again.

Australia has some amazing animals. **Platypuses** are mammals, but lay eggs. The **koala** is good at climbing gum trees to eat the leaves. Koalas have finger prints that look like human finger prints!

2 Aborigines have lived in Australia for a very long time. They learned to make all they needed from the land, plants and animals. This man is playing a '**didgeridoo**' – it is a musical instrument made from a long hollow branch.

3 The Great Barrier Reef is the biggest coral reef in the world. Visitors love to see the wonderful sea life by scuba-diving or looking through a glass-bottomed boat.

4 **Melbourne is the main city of the state of Victoria.** Australia has 7 states – can you find them on the map? All the biggest cities of Australia are near the sea.

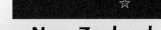

Australia	New Zealand

SURPRISE! There's a flag from page 13 on these flags! The stars show the 'Southern Cross'. Can you see the differences?*

5 **Kiwis live in New Zealand.** These birds do not fly but come out at night and look for grubs to eat.

Can you find fruit from New Zealand? Look in shops for the labels.

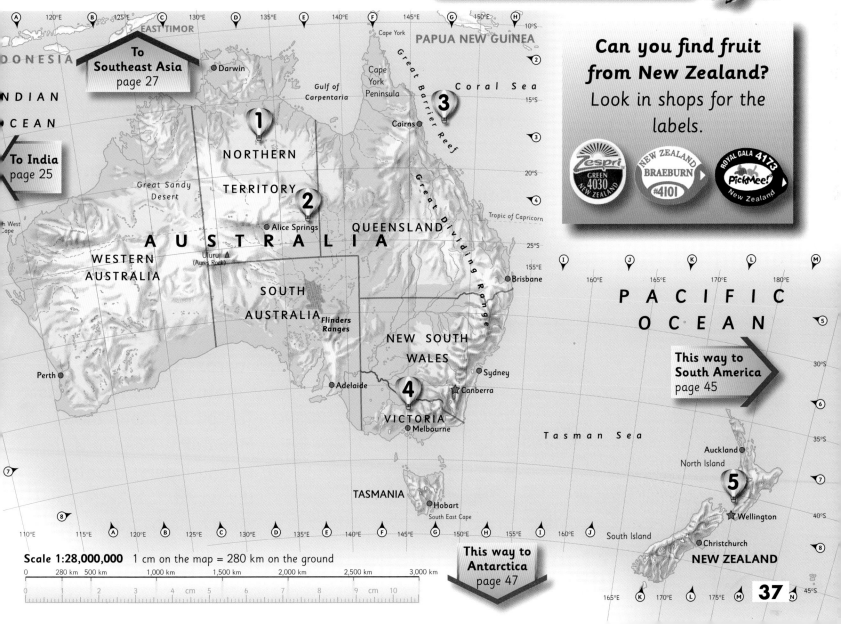

To Southeast Asia
page 27

To India
page 25

EAST TIMOR

DONESIA

NDIAN

CEAN

Darwin

Gulf of Carpentaria

Cape York

PAPUA NEW GUINEA

Cape York Peninsula

Coral Sea

Cairns

Great Barrier Reef

1

3

NORTHERN

TERRITORY

Great Sandy Desert

2

Alice Springs

QUEENSLAND

Tropic of Capricorn

A U S T R A L I A

Uluru (Ayres Rock)

WESTERN

AUSTRALIA

SOUTH

AUSTRALIA

Flinders Ranges

Great Dividing Range

Brisbane

P A C I F I C

O C E A N

NEW SOUTH

WALES

Perth

Adelaide

4

Sydney

Canberra

VICTORIA

Melbourne

Tasman Sea

This way to South America page 45

Auckland
North Island

TASMANIA

Hobart
South East Cape

South Island

5

Wellington

Christchurch

NEW ZEALAND

Scale 1:28,000,000   1 cm on the map = 280 km on the ground

0   280 km   500 km   1,000 km   1,500 km   2,000 km   2,500 km   3,000 km

This way to Antarctica page 47

Discover...
Canada and Alaska

1 **Alaska has amazing wildlife, like this Alaskan grizzly bear.** Alaska is part of the USA: the USA bought it from Russia in 1867. It is near Russia and partly in the Arctic. In winter it is very cold and days are short.

Do you know any Native American words?
Canada means 'village' in Mohawk.
Kayak is a boat like a canoe.
Wigwam and **Teepee**: these are types of tent.

2 **There is oil in Alaska.** This is an oil terminal on the Alaskan coast. Can you see 2 big tankers (ships)?

3 **This train travels right across Canada, over plains and mountains.** This picture shows the Rocky Mountains. Canada is the second biggest country in the world. It takes 4 days for a train to travel from one side to the other!

RUSSIA

70°N 80°N 160°W 140°W 120°W 100°W 80°W 60°N 40°W 80°N 70°N 10°W

A R C T I C   O C E A N

20°W

ATLANTIC
OCEAN

GREENLAND
(Denmark)

ICELAND

Denmark Strait

Bering Strait

Beaufort
Sea

Queen Elizabeth Islands

McClure Strait

Baffin
Bay

Davis Strait

Arctic Circle

30°N

**To the
North Pole**
page 46

Bering
Sea

Yukon

Arctic Circle

Alaska
(USA)

Mount McKinley

Anchorage

Alaska Range

Alaska Peninsula

Victoria
Island

N U N A V U T

Baffin
Island

60°N

40°N

**This way
to Europe**
page 15

Gulf of
Alaska

YUKON
TERRITORY

Whitehorse

NORTHWEST
TERRITORIES

Yellowknife

Hudson Strait

Labrador Sea

NEWFOUNDLAND
AND
LABRADOR

**This way
to Asia**
page 29

Skagway

50°N

PACIFIC OCEAN

Hudson
Bay

Labrador

Labrador
City

St John's
Newfoundland

**Look at the
map.** Can you
see the Rocky
Mountains
stretching down
the western side
of Canada and
into the USA?

BRITISH
COLUMBIA

ALBERTA

C A N A D A

SASKATCHEWAN

MANITOBA

Lake
Winnipeg

O N T A R I O

Q U E B E C

Gulf of
St Lawrence

PRINCE
EDWARD
ISLAND

NOVA SCOTIA

Halifax

St Lawrence

Fraser

Rocky Mountains

Vancouver
Island

Vancouver

Calgary

Victoria

Regina

Winnipeg

Lake
Superior

NEW
BRUNSWICK

Fredericton

Quebec

Quebec
City

Cape Sable

60°N

Montreal

Ottawa

Lake
Huron

Toronto

Lake
Ontario

Niagara Falls

Lake Erie

ATLANTIC
OCEAN

40°N

Lake Michigan

U N I T E D   S T A T E S   O F   A M E R I C A

140°W 130°W 120°W 110°W 100°W 90°W 80°W 70°W

Scale 1:30,000,000   1 cm on the map = 300 km on the ground

0   300 km   1,000 km   1,500 km   2,000 km   2,500 km   3,000 km   3,500 km

0   1   2   3   4   cm   6   7   8   9   cm   10   11

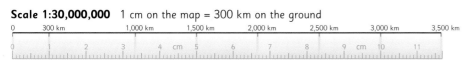

**The Canadian flag has
a red maple leaf on it.**
In autumn the maple
leaves turn red. Some
people say the hills turn
red like fire.

4 **The
Niagara
Falls are shared by
Canada and the USA.**
They are between Lake
Erie and Lake Ontario.

5 **Newfoundland
was named when
Europeans 'found' it.**
This fishing village is
MUCH closer to Europe
than to western Canada!

Discover...
The USA

1 The Statue of Liberty was a gift from France over 100 years ago. It stands on an island in New York's harbour, and welcomes people who arrive by sea.

The bald eagle – America's national bird. This eagle is not really bald! The feathers on its head are pure white. It feeds on fish, mainly salmon.

2 Harvesting wheat. Large machines called combine harvesters, like the red one in this picture, are used to harvest the grain.

3 Monument Valley. These amazing sandstone formations are in the Arizona desert. They are **huge**! Can you see a car at the bottom of the picture?

Can you . . . find a long river with a long name on the map?* Here's a clue: •ISS•SSI••I

(Hint!)

4 The oldest living thing on Earth?

Bristlecone pine trees live for a very long time. Some of them are about 5,000 years old.

5 A tram station in downtown San Diego.

Trams are a great way to travel in cities: they travel fast on rails and they are clean and quiet.

Did you know?

The names of states tell us about the origins of the peoples of America:
Vermont – means 'green mountain' (French).
Nevada – means 'snowy' (Spanish).
Iowa – means 'beautiful land' (American Indian).

Scale 1:21,500,000   1 cm on the map = 215 km on the ground

| 0 | 215 km | 500 km | 1,000 km | 1,500 km | 2,000 km | 2,500 km |

To Canada and Alaska page 39

This way to Europe page 15

To the Pacific page 35

To Central America page 43

MASS = Massachusetts
CONN = Connecticut

UNITED STATES OF AMERICA

PACIFIC OCEAN

ATLANTIC OCEAN

Gulf of Mexico

MEXICO

BAHAMAS

Discover...
Central America

Mexico is a big country. Mexico City is one of the biggest and busiest cities in the world. There are big deserts, mountains and volcanoes in Mexico.

2 **This rare bird lives in the rainforests of Central America.** It is a **quetzal**. A lot of the wildlife in the forests is very special, so it is important to look after the forests for the wildlife.

NORTH AMERICA
Atlantic Ocean
Panama Canal
Pacific Ocean
SOUTH AMERICA

4 **The flag of Jamaica:**
Green – for farming
Gold – for sunshine
Black – for hardship

3 **The Panama Canal is amazing – and useful too!** Big ships can go from the **Pacific Ocean** to the **Atlantic Ocean**. How do you think ships could get from the Pacific to the Atlantic Ocean before this canal was dug?* Do you think it took a long time? The globe will help you!

6 **A carnival procession on Curaçao.** These women are enjoying a colourful street carnival. **SURPRISE!** Curaçao is a **Dutch** island.

Maize first came from Central America. Now it is grown all over the world. As well as corn-on-the-cob and sweetcorn, it is used for cornflakes and popcorn, and its flour is used in tortillas.

5 **So many islands!** Tourists can travel on a ship and visit one island every day in the Caribbean. But beware of **hurricanes**!

Bananas grow fast. This stamp shows bananas growing. Look hard at the stamp .... **Can you see** the green bananas growing – upwards?

On the map there is an island with **2** countries on it. In the west they speak **French**, but in the east they speak **Spanish**. What are the countries called?*

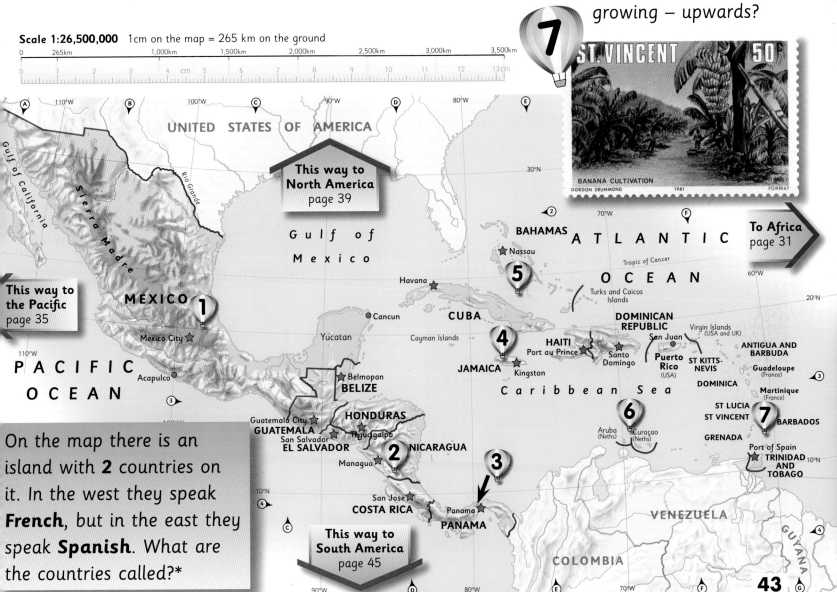

Scale 1:26,500,000   1cm on the map = 265 km on the ground

ST. VINCENT 50¢
BANANA CULTIVATION
GORDON DRUMMOND   1981   FORMAT

7

UNITED STATES OF AMERICA

This way to North America page 39

Gulf of California
Rio Grande
Sierra Madre

This way to the Pacific page 35

MEXICO **1**
Mexico City
Acapulco

PACIFIC OCEAN

Gulf of Mexico

Havana
Cancun
Yucatan
Cayman Islands

CUBA

BAHAMAS
Nassau

ATLANTIC OCEAN

To Africa page 31

Tropic of Cancer

Turks and Caicos Islands

DOMINICAN REPUBLIC
Santo Domingo
San Juan
Virgin Islands (USA and UK)
Puerto Rico (USA)

HAITI
Port au Prince
4
JAMAICA
Kingston

ST KITTS-NEVIS
ANTIGUA AND BARBUDA
Guadeloupe (France)
DOMINICA
Martinique (France)

Caribbean Sea

Belmopan
BELIZE
Guatemala City
GUATEMALA
San Salvador
EL SALVADOR
HONDURAS
Tegucigalpa
2 NICARAGUA
Managua

San Jose
COSTA RICA
3
Panama
PANAMA

6
Aruba (Neths)
Curaçao (Neths)

ST LUCIA
ST VINCENT
GRENADA
Port of Spain
TRINIDAD AND TOBAGO

7 BARBADOS

VENEZUELA

COLOMBIA

GUYANA

This way to South America page 45

Discover... South America

1 **A giant tortoise on the Galapagos Islands.** These volcanic islands are very far from other land. As a result, many special animals and plants only live here. **Can you** guess the age of the oldest giant tortoise?*

3 **Lake Titicaca is high up in the Andes.** These boats are made from reeds (surprise!), and they do float. It is so high up here that visitors get out of breath. **Can you** see which 2 countries share the lake?*

2 **The Amazon jungle is hot and wet.** The river is called the Amazon too! The trees are very big. There are so many different animals and plants here that no-one has ever seen them all. But some of the jungle is being chopped down.

4 **Buenos Aires.** This is the capital city of a big country – can you find it on the map?* 'Buenos Aires' means 'good air' in Spanish.

5 **The Atacama Desert in Chile.** This is the driest place in the world. The desert is very hot and dry. But the high Andes mountains are cold – with snow!

Which is the biggest cat in South America? It is the **jaguar**! Most jaguars live in the lowland rainforests near the Amazon River.

6 This is a '**monkey puzzle tree**'. It grows in the south of Chile – its real name is a '**Chilean pine**'. **Is it chilly in Chile?** Sometimes! It is cold in the high mountains and in the south of Chile. But it is hot in the desert and in the summer (December) in central Chile.

Can you find how many countries touch Brazil?*

This way to the USA page 41

This way to the Pacific page 35

This way to Africa page 31

This way to Antarctica page 47

MEXICO
BELIZE
GUATEMALA
HONDURAS
EL SALVADOR
NICARAGUA
COSTA RICA
PANAMA
CUBA
JAMAICA
HAITI
DOMINICAN REPUBLIC
Caribbean Sea
Caracas
TRINIDAD AND TOBAGO
VENEZUELA
Orinoco
Georgetown
GUYANA
Paramaribo
SURINAME
Cayenne
FRENCH GUYANA
Bogota
COLOMBIA
Guiana Highlands
Negro
Galapagos Islands (Ecuador)
Quito
ECUADOR
Amazon
Manaus
Amazon
Amazon Basin
B R A Z I L
P E R U
Lima
Lake Titicaca
La Paz
BOLIVIA
Brasilia
Brazilian Highlands
São Francisco
Atacama Desert
PARAGUAY
Asuncion
Parana
Rio de Janeiro
Sao Paulo
PACIFIC OCEAN
ATLANTIC OCEAN
Tropic of Capricorn
CHILE
Valparaiso
Santiago
Juan Fernandez Islands (Chile)
Buenos Aires
URUGUAY
Montevideo
Rio de la Plata
ARGENTINA
Patagonia
Falkland Islands (UK)
Stanley
South Georgia (UK)
Cape Horn
Equator

Scale 1:44,000,000 1 cm on the map = 440 km on the ground

0   440 km   1,000 km   2,000 km   3,000 km   4,000 km   5,000 km

0   1   2   3   4   cm   5   6   7   8   9   cm   10   11

Discover...
The Arctic

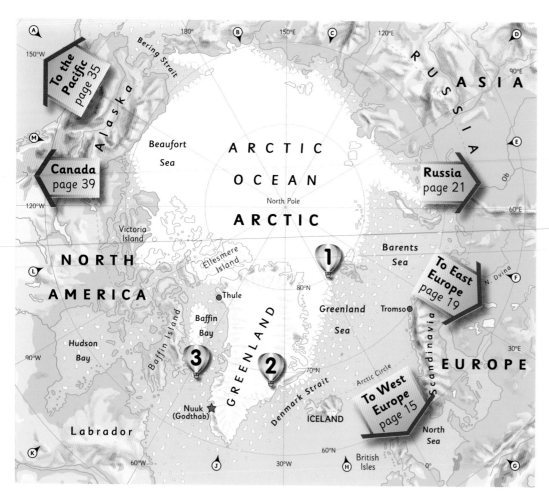

Map labels

150°W · 180° · 150°E · 120°E · 90°E

A · B · C · D · E

To the Pacific page 35

Bering Strait

Alaska

M

Beaufort Sea

Canada page 39

ARCTIC OCEAN

North Pole

ARCTIC

Victoria Island

120°W

60°E

Russia page 21

RUSSIA ASIA

Ob

N. Dvina

F

NORTH AMERICA

Ellesmere Island

L

Thule

80°N

Greenland Sea

Tromso

Barents Sea

To East Europe page 19

Baffin Island

Baffin Bay

Hudson Bay

90°W

GREENLAND

70°N

Denmark Strait

Arctic Circle

Scandinavia

EUROPE

30°E

To West Europe page 15

Nuuk (Godthab)

ICELAND

North Sea

Labrador

K

60°W

J

30°W

60°N

H

British Isles

0°

G

Scale 1:50,000,000   1 cm on the map = 500 km on the ground

0 · 500 km · 1,000 km · 2,000 km · 4,000 km · 6,000 km · 8,000 km · 10,000 km

0 · 1 · 2 · 3 · 4 cm · 5 · 6 · 7 · 8 · 9 cm · 10 · 11 · 12

Stamps

KALAALLIT NUNAAT   WWF   *Uppik Sneugle Nyctea scandiaca*   GRØNLAND 4.75

KALAALLIT NUNAAT   *Uppik Sneugle Nyctea scandiaca*   GRØNLAND 5.50

Greenland is mostly white with ice, not green! These owls are white so they are hard to see in the snow.

AMAZING! In the **ARCTIC**, there are 24 hours of **daylight** in **June** and 24 hours of **darkness** in **December**.

1 Polar bears live in the Arctic. They are the biggest of all the bears. They hunt for fish and seals.

3 People live in the Arctic. This Inuit hunter and his dogsled team are travelling on the frozen polar sea of Baffin Bay.

Discover... Antarctica

1 Penguins live in the **Antarctic**. They can't fly but they are brilliant swimmers.

AMAZING! In the **ANTARCTIC**, there are 24 hours of **darkness** in **June** and 24 hours of **daylight** in **December**.

2 Can you name these flags? They are some of the countries that have bases in Antarctica.*

3 Some tourists come to see Antarctica by boat. Beware of icebergs!

4
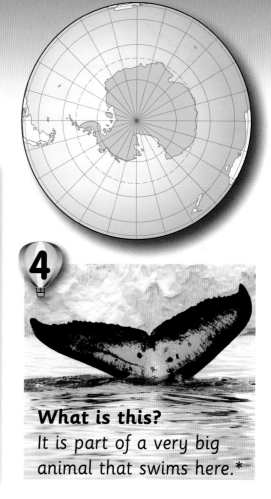

What is this? It is part of a very big animal that swims here.*

Scale **1:50,000,000**   1 cm on the map = 500 km on the ground

0	500 km	1,000 km	2,000 km	4,000 km	6,000 km	8,000 km	10,000 km

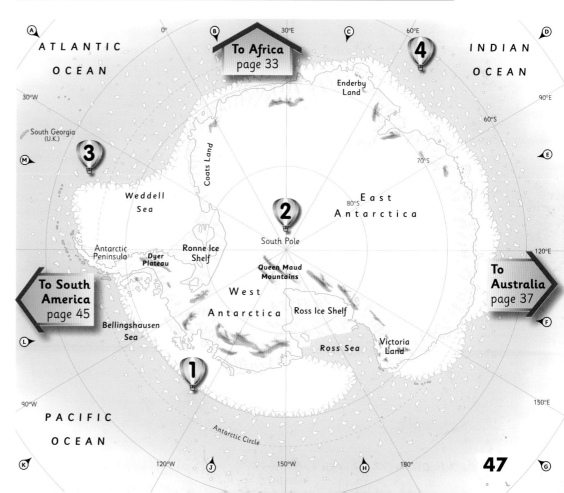

ATLANTIC OCEAN

To Africa page 33

INDIAN OCEAN

Enderby Land

South Georgia (U.K.)

Coats Land

Weddell Sea

East Antarctica

South Pole

Antarctic Peninsula

Dyer Plateau

Ronne Ice Shelf

Queen Maud Mountains

To South America page 45

West Antarctica

Ross Ice Shelf

Bellingshausen Sea

Victoria Land

Ross Sea

To Australia page 37

PACIFIC OCEAN

Antarctic Circle

Index

Answers to Questions

Page 10 USA, Brazil and Nigeria.

Page 19 New countries are Estonia, Latvia, Lithuania, Belarus, Ukraine, Moldova, Czech Republic, Slovak Republic, Slovenia, Croatia, Bosnia, Serbia, Montenegro, Kosovo, Macedonia. 2 big seas are Baltic and Black.

Page 21 The Caspian Sea is shared by Russia, Kazakhstan, Turkmenistan, Azerbaijan and Iran.

Page 22 The three continents are Africa, Asia and Europe.

Page 23 The biggest country is Saudi Arabia. The stamp shows 2 palm trees, 3 fruit trees, farmland, a village and a tower.

Page 33 Lake Tanganyika and Lake Malawi.

Page 37 Australia's flag has 6 stars. New Zealand's flag has 4 stars.

Page 40 Mississippi River.

Page 42 Ships had to go all the way around South America. See map on page 45.

Page 43 In Haiti the people speak French – in the Dominican Republic people speak Spanish.

Page 44 The oldest giant tortoise was 152 years old. Lake Titicaca is shared by Peru and Bolivia. Buenos Aires is the capital city of Argentina.

Page 45 10 countries touch Brazil.

Page 47 The flags are from New Zealand, Chile, Norway, Argentina, United Kingdom and France. The picture is of the tail of a whale.

Photo Acknowledgements

Robin Aiello (Ocean Antics Consulting) 36 centre bottom; **Alamy** /Ashley Cooper 13 top left, /David Lomax/Robert Harding Picture Library Ltd 14 top left, /Zaichiki 18 bottom left, /Bert de Ruiter 18 bottom right, /Iain Masterton 20 top right, /Oleg Moiseyenko 20 bottom left, / Dinodia Images 25 top left, /FAN travelstock 30 centre left, /Friedrich Stark 31 centre right, /Images&Stories 32 top left, /Images of Africa Photobank 31 top right, /FAN travelstock 30 centre left, /Friedrich Stark 31 centre right, /Terry Fincher.Photo Int 38 top right, /Images Etc Ltd 38 bottom, /blickwinkel 41 top left, /Ambient Images Inc. 41 top centre, /World Pictures 42 top left, / VI 43 top centre, /JUPITERIMAGES/Creatas 44 top left, /Mireille Vautier 44 bottom left, /Chad Ehlers 44 bottom right; **City of Johannesburg** / Walter Knirr 33 top right; **Corbis** /Gabe Palmer/zefa 2 centre right, /Image Plan (RF) 6 montage top left, /Image100 (RF) 6 montage top right, /Robert Glusic (RF) 6 montage bottom left, /Kristi J. Black (RF) 6 montage bottom right, /Pawel Libera 12 top left, /Felix Ordonez/Reuters 16 top left, /David Turnley 18 top left, /Kevin Burke 18 bottom centre, /Goodshoot 20 top left, /Atef Hassan/Reuters 22 bottom left, /Reuters 23 top left, /Paul Almasy 24 top left, /Steven Vidler/Eurasia Press 25 top right, /Jacques Langevin 28 top left, /Keren Su 28 centre right, /Yann Arthus-Bertrand 30 top left, /Bruno Fert 31 bottom left, /Paul Almasy 30 top left, /George Steinmetz 34 centre left, /Paul A. Souders 36 top right, /Claire Leimbach/Robert Harding World Imagery 36 top right, /Erwin & Peggy Bauer/zefa 38 top left, /Danny Lehman 42 centre left, /DLILLC (RF) 46 bottom left, /Layne Kennedy 46 bottom right; **Dreamstime.com** /Gibbsterr 12 top right, /Railpix 12 bottom left, /Lastdays1 14 bottom left, /Kurt 14 bottom right, /Britvich 15 centre left, / Gnugent 17 centre left, /Dmitryp 20 bottom right, /Nalukai 35 top left, / Lesterlester 44 bottom left, /Eg004713 45 top left, /Wildernessphotographs 45 centre left, /Bernardbreton 47 bottom left, /Cascoly 47 centre; **Fotolia. com** /bobroy20 16 bottom right, /RadioUran 21 top left, /Alena Yakusheva 26 bottom left (and back cover), /jorisvo 29 top left, /Stephan Karg 30 bottom centre, /robert paul van beets 37 top left; **iStockphoto.com** / Rolf Weschke 13 top right, /Daniel Breckwoldt 15 top left, /Branislav Bubanja 16 bottom left, /Ricardo De Mattos 17 top left, /Angelafoto 17 top right, /Ferenc Vágvölgyi 19 bottom left, /Andrey Kolganov 20 centre, /Rob Broek 21 top right, /Steven Allan 22 top left, /Alena Yakusheva 22 bottom left, /David Ciemny 24 bottom left, /x-drew 24 bottom right, /Robert Churchill 26 top left, /Martyn Smith 26 bottom right, /Paolo Santoné 27 top right, /Alan Tobey 28 bottom left, /Ralph Paprzycki 29 top right, /Richard Gunion 33 bottom centre, /Allan Morrison 39 bottom right, /Tony Campbell 40 centre left, /Steve Geer 43 top left, /Mark Fitzsimmons 47 top right; **NASA/GSFC** /Reto Stockli, Alan Nelson, Fritz Hasler 6 top; **NPA Satellite Mapping (www.npa.cgg.com)** 5 bottom, 8 top; **Caroline Ohara** 40 bottom left; **Oxford Scientific (OSF)** /Paulo de Oliveira 34 top left; **Shutterstock** /leonello calvetti front cover globe, /achinthamb 40 top left.

Glossary

Have fun with this page: match the pictures on this page with pictures in the main atlas.

 **Border** – the line where 2 countries meet. Borders are shown as red lines on the maps.

 **Canal** – a man-made river, dug by people for boats to travel on. Spot one on page 42.

 **Capital city** – the city where the government of the country meets. This city is on page 42.

 **Continent** – the largest areas of land. There are 7 continents on Earth, shown on page 10.

 Coral – tiny sea animals; when they die their shells become like rocks. Pages 34 and 36.

 **Country** – an area of land that is ruled by its own government.

 **Crops** – plants grown by people to use for food. See how many crops you can find in this atlas. Try pages 17, 18, 25, 26, 32, 40 and 43.

 **Desert** – a big area of land where it is very, very dry. Find deserts on pages 30, 40 and 45.

 **Farming** – using land to grow crops or keep animals, usually for food.

 **Globe** – a map of the world that is printed on a sphere (ball shape). Find a globe on page 1 and page 7.

 **Irrigation** – watering crops to keep the plants alive. You can find this stamp on page 23.

 **Lake** – an area of water that is surrounded by land. Find this lake on page 20.

 **Mining** – digging up things people want from under the ground. See page 33.

 **Mountains** – land which is high, and usually steep and rocky too. See mountains on pages 13, 15, 24, 38 and 45.

 **Oasis** – a place in a desert where there is water. See page 30.

 **Pollution** – when people put things into the air, soil or water that make them dirty and not safe.

 **Transport** – moving people or things. How many different sorts of transport can you find in this Atlas?

 **Tundra** – land in the far north where it is so cold it is always frozen underneath. See page 21.

 **Volcano** – a mountain with a hole in the top that sometimes sends out melted rock (lava), in a sudden explosion. See page 34.

Country flags from around the World

 Lebanon

 **Lesotho**

 Liberia

 **Libya**

 Liechtenstein

 Lithuania

 Luxembou

 Marshall Islands

 Mauritania

 **Mauritius**

 **Mexico**

 **Micronesia**

 **Moldova**

 **Monac**

 Netherlands

 **New Zealand**

 Nicaragua

 Niger

 **Nigeria**

 Northern Marianas

 Norwa

 Poland

 Portugal

 **Puerto Rico**

 **Qatar**

 Romania

 Russia

 Rwand

 Singapore

 Slovak Republic

 **Slovenia**

 Solomon Islands

 Somalia

 South Africa

 Spain

 Swaziland

 Sweden

 Switzerland

 Syria

 Taiwan

 Tajikistan

 Tanzani

 **Tuvalu**

 Uganda

 Ukraine

 **United Arab Emirates**

 **United Kingdom**

United States of America

Urugua